Santa's Scenic

written and illustrated by
Misty McNally

*dedicated to my husband
and to Iowa children of all ages*

ISBN 978-1-937881-00-9

© Copyright 2011 Kate Shelley Publishing
Reproduction in whole or in part without express written
permission of the publisher is strictly prohibited.

Printed in the USA by Boelte-Hall, Roeland Park, KS

Long ago in "Ioway" in your great-great-grandpa's day
'twas a wild and unsettled place
of rolling plains and open space
where grasses grew high as a tall man's brows
and more deer roamed the hills than pigs and cows.
Children of settlers played in the knolls,
catching their suppers with fishing poles,
hiding-and-seeking behind the maples
and tending the animals in the stables.

Summers were filled with fragrant blossoms,
the creeks were tramped by raccoons and possums,
songbirds trilled from forest treetops,
and fields were green with sprouting crops.
A big river flowed there, wide and serene,
and a tall train trestle crossed the ravine.
So pretty the view was, so rolling and hilly,
the people there named it the Scenic Valley.

One winter, snow fell deep and thick,
the ice on the river froze hard and slick,
the sky turned dark and the wind blew ill,
and a Christmas Eve blizzard brought bitter chill.

The temperature dropped to thirty below,
the fields were piled with ten feet of snow,
and even reindeer could not fly
through the swirling storm that filled the sky.

Out on the plains on the rugged frontier
in a little log home built by pioneers,
five children said prayers that Christmas Eve night
as their Ma and Pa tucked them in tight.

Then snug under quilts, each child made one wish—
Jack wanted a pole for catching fish,
Mary asked for a tea set, and James, a bright top,
then Maggie, a red-and-white striped lollipop,
and last but not least, the oldest child, Kate,
dreamed of a pair of real ice skates.

Up at the Pole, Santa worried and wondered,
fussed and fretted, pouted, and pondered,
"How will I get gifts to the children in cabins?"
Santa said to himself, "How will Christmas happen?
The skies are too risky to fly my reindeer,
the wind too wild, the cold too severe!"

He said,
"Something stronger must carry my loads that can plow through the snow and doesn't need roads, made of iron and steel with muscle and might that can conquer the blizzard and get through the night."

Then away in the distance a train whistle blew, and suddenly Santa knew what to do. "They'll have their gifts by Christmastide! **I'll take the Scenic Valley Ride!**"

To hide who he was and divert prying eyes
Santa covered his red suit with a disguise—
a stovepipe hat and a long black coat
plus a fluffy knit muffler wrapped 'round his throat.
Then he stuffed all the gifts into duffles and sacks
and trunks and bags, and rushed down to the tracks.

When he came to the station
he stopped in the cold
for there on the rails
was a sight to behold—
a HUGE
LOCOMOTIVE

shiny and
gleaming
with brakes
a-hissing and
smokestack
steaming,
each piston and hitch
and axle and wheel
mightily forged
from shimmering steel,
black and bright gold,
arrayed like a king,
with a brass bell that rang
DING-DING, DING-DING

and a moon-like headlamp shone bright white,
cutting a slice through the ink of the night.

Santa raced to the window to purchase a ticket,
gave the agent his nickels, then lickety-splicket
the porters escorted him, lugging his packs

under their arms and over their backs,
throwing each sack on the rack with a heave,
and then just as the train was starting to leave...

The Scenic Conductor soon came up the aisle,
with his yellow-rimmed cap and a wide, toothy smile.
He looked Santa over in his disguise,
saw his piles of packs, then winked one of his eyes.
He took Santa's ticket and snipped it,
CLIP,
tipped his hat and then said, "Have a nice trip!"

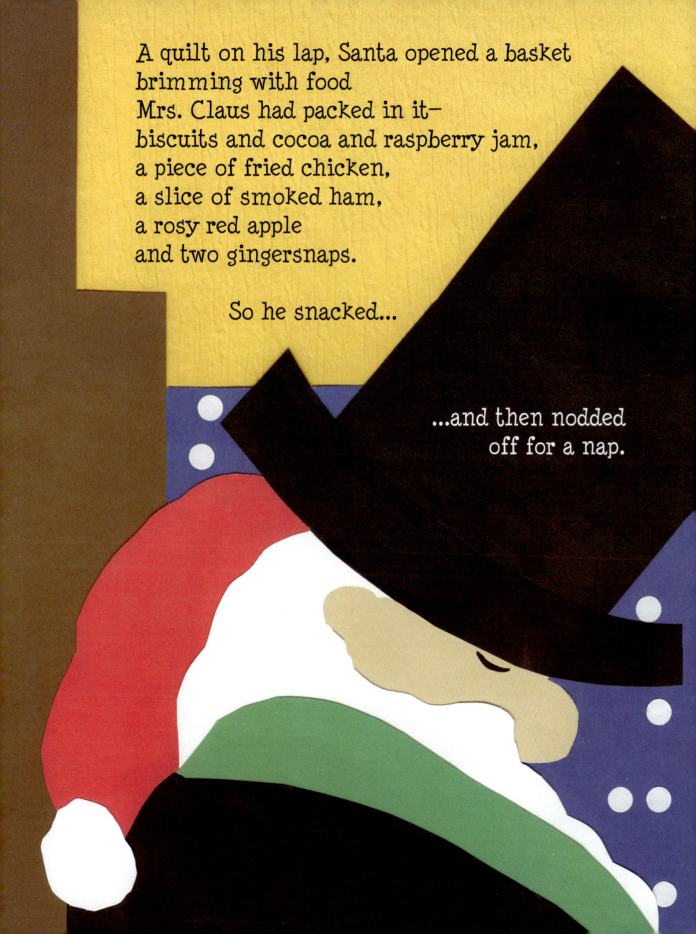

Suddenly Santa was jolted from sleep—
the train was stuck in a snowdrift deep!
A mountain of baggage spilled from the racks,
onto the floor and out of the packs,
so there in the aisle the presents were piled—
every good gift for every good child!

There were bags of hard candies
and ropes you could skip,
a miniature train and a tiny wood ship,
glass ornaments and baskets of fruit
an Indian drum and a little reed flute.
There were tiny tin soldiers and books to be read,
windup toys and a quilt for a bed,
licorice drops and striped candy canes
and jingle bells for a horse's sleigh reins.

Santa hurried and scurried to repack the gifts
as the railroad workers surveyed the drifts.
Then with shovels and picks,
they started to dig
and with singing and slinging,
uncovered the rig.

Again the Line chugged along the train track
with a regular rhythm of clickety-clack.
Having hidden the gifts, Santa breathed a deep sigh,
watching blanketed fields and forests rush by,
looking through Jack-Frosty, fogged window glass
as the snow whooshed up through the air as they passed.

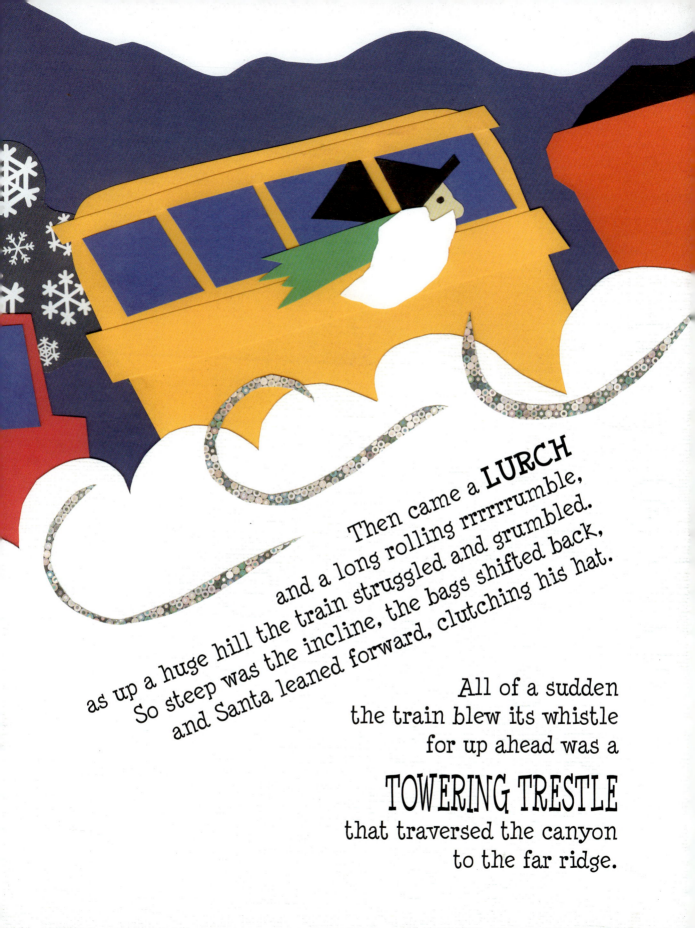

Then came a **LURCH**
and a long rolling rrrrrrumble,
as up a huge hill the train struggled and grumbled.
So steep was the incline, the bags shifted back,
and Santa leaned forward, clutching his hat.

All of a sudden
the train blew its whistle
for up ahead was a

TOWERING TRESTLE

that traversed the canyon
to the far ridge.

It was the
Scenic Valley High Bridge,
so long across and so tall in height
that all aboard were amazed at the sight!
Santa peered out the fogged-up window and
shivered
for far below was a wide, frozen river.
A serpent of silver, it slithered and shined,
crawling the carpeted valley of pines.

Reaching the far side, the Scenic Ride rallied, plunging with speed down the steep-sided valley. The engine was steaming and cars were careening with Santa and packages bouncing and leaning.

The blizzard then stopped, the full moon was bright, and the sparkling snow was glittering white.

In spite of the snow and to Santa's delight,
the train was on time—Christmas Eve at midnight!

When the Scenic arrived
on that Iowa frontier
it awakened the
children of pioneers.
They heard the whistle
and jumped out of bed
hoping that Santa had come,
but instead

they saw an old man
in a tophat and coat
with bags on his back
and a beard like a goat

rushing away through
the newfallen snow,
giggling and jiggling and
laughing, "HO HO!"

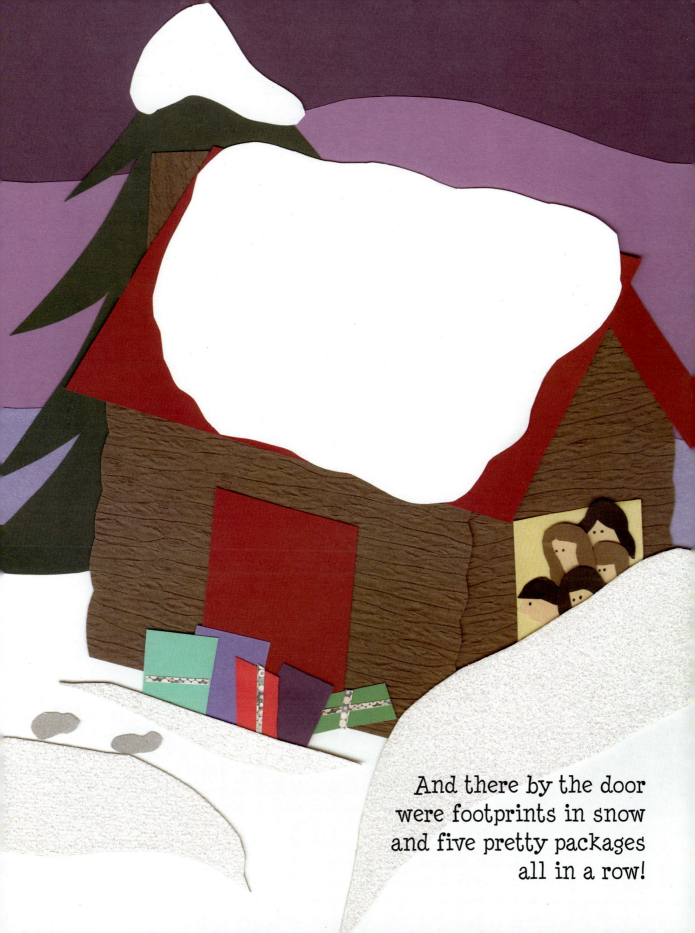

And there by the door were footprints in snow and five pretty packages all in a row!

That snowy Christmas, as each child wished,
Jack got a pole for catching fish.
Mary, a tea set, and James, a bright top,
and Maggie, a red-and-white striped lollipop,
and last but not least, with a tag that said "Kate"
was a beautiful pair of new ice skates.

And home at the Pole, Santa nodded and smiled
for every good gift was with every good child.
Then he sipped on his cocoa and sighed, satisfied,
reliving the memory of his Scenic train ride.

So that's how, my children, long ago
in Ioway in the blizzard and snow,
Santa took the Scenic Line
and a train, not reindeer, brought Christmastime,
and in Scenic Valley in a one-room cabin,
five children had gifts

and Christmas did happen.

This book was inspired by the magnificent trains, high bridges, and spectacular views in Boone, Iowa, and along the Boone & Scenic Valley Railroad. The children in the story—Kate, James, Mary, Maggie, and John (Jack)—are named for the young Boone railway heroine of 1881, Kate Shelley, and her siblings.

For more about the Boone & Scenic Valley Railroad, the life of Kate Shelley, the High Bridges of Boone, or the rich railroad history of Iowa, contact:

Kate Shelley Publishing
www.KateShelley.com
(816) 260-7663

Boone & Scenic Valley Railroad
James H. Andrew Museum
225 10th Street, Boone, Iowa 50036
www.scenic-valleyrr.com
(800) 626-0319

To learn more about Iowa's railroad heroine, read:

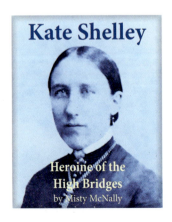

KATE SHELLEY
Heroine of the High Bridges
by Misty McNally

available at www.KateShelley.com